Praise God with Paper Bags

Anita Reith Stohs

Illustrated by Becky Radtke

CONCORDIA PUBLISHING HOUSE · SAINT LOUIS

To Reuben and Jayne Stohs,
who have run the race well.
Hebrews 12:1—2

Published by Concordia Publishing House
3558 S. Jefferson Avenue
St. Louis, MO 63118-3968

This publication may be available in braille, in large print, or on cassette tape for the visually impaired. Please allow 8 to 12 weeks for delivery. Write to the Library for the Blind, 1333 S. Kirkwood Rd., St. Louis, MO 63122-7295; call 1-800-433-3954, ext. 1322; or e-mail to blind.library@lcms.org.

Manufactured in the United States of America

1   2   3   4   5   6   7   8   9   10   13   12   11   10   09   08   07   06   05   04

Contents

Index of Bible Stories

Introduction

Class time is fast approaching! You need a quick teaching aid to help tell a Bible story or you want an inexpensive craft to show your students how the lesson applies to their daily lives as Christians. A solution is as close as a paper bag.

Pull out a bag and peek in this book for a fast and easy solution.

The projects described here are intended to provide you with simple, inexpensive crafts to introduce a lesson, tell a Bible story, or apply its Gospel point to a student's life. Basic instructions are simple with additional creative options provided, as well as suggestions for specific Bible stories or themes with which the projects can be used. Reproducible patterns are included. And a drawing of how each finished craft might look serves as a guide and a jumping-off point for your students' creative expression.

As much as possible, have children draw their own faces, shapes, and figures for the crafts. Using God's gift of creativity helps children of all ages express themselves and learn more about the world He made.

Useful suggestions for creating with paper bags*

1 Brown and white bags are readily available at grocery and discount stores. Colored paper bags are often found at craft stores.

2 If you have the time and facilities, decorate bags with tempera or craft paint instead of crayons and markers.

3 To make projects more durable, spray with acrylic craft shellac, paint with a mixture of equal parts white glue and water, or glue two or more layers of paper together.

4 Crush paper then flatten it again to make it more flexible for stuffing.

5 To make paper resemble leather or parchment, crumple the paper bag then smooth it out by hand and with an iron.

6 When drawing on brown paper, experiment with the colors and media to determine what shows up best and gives you the desired result.

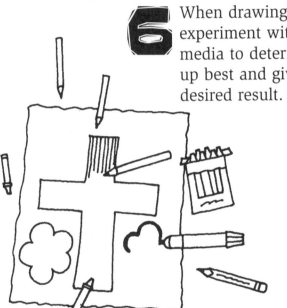

7 Use a photocopier to enlarge or reduce symbols and patterns provided in this book.

These projects were developed for use with children in preschool and lower elementary classes in Sunday school, day school, home school, or camp. They can also be used with children who have developmental disabilities. Several projects were designed with the help of young adults with developmental disabilities. Lesson Connections were developed with the assistance of CPH editors.

May the Holy Spirit be with you as you use the projects in this book to lead the children in your care to Jesus, their loving Savior.

The Author

Angel

What You Need

White lunch bag
Scissors
Glue
White yarn or ribbon
Paper

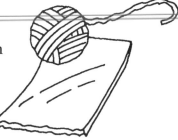

What You Do

1. Cut off the front of the paper bag so you have a rectangle. Twist it then smooth it out.

2. Fold the rectangle in half and tie yarn or ribbon around the center, leaving a few inches for a hanger.

3. Roll a small paper ball and fit it inside the middle of the fold. Tie off the paper below the fold to form a head.

4. Cut a piece from the remaining portion of the paper bag. Twist it, then smooth it out, then twist one time at the center to form wings.

5. Glue the center twist of the wings under the angel's head. With yarn or ribbon, tie a waist below the wings.

6. Trim the wings as desired.

7. Hang the angel from the ceiling or use it as a Christmas ornament.

More to Do

1. Use fabric trim, glitter glue or fabric paint to add details to the angel.

2. Instead of yarn or ribbon use raffia or metallic cording.

3. Omit the hanger and glue a craft stick into the bottom of the angel to make a stick puppet.

4. Make an angel as a visual aid, room decoration, or take-home activity for one of the many Bible stories in which angels are mentioned.

The Lesson Connection

The Annunciation: Luke 1:6–38

"You will give birth to a son," an angel told Mary. "He will be God's Son, and you are to give Him the name Jesus." A faithful Jewish girl, Mary undoubtedly felt great joy and awe at this news because it meant the Old Testament prophecies about the Messiah were coming true—through her! Make this angel decoration as a reminder of the birth of Jesus, our Savior, whose life, death, and resurrection brought fulfillment to God's promises.

Other Lesson Connections
Advent and Christmas
An angel appears to Zechariah
An angel appears to Joseph
Angels appear to the shepherds
An angel appears to the Wise Men
The flight to Egypt

He Comes

What You Need

Paper bag
Scissors
Glue
Yarn
Dowel
Construction paper
Markers

What You Do

1. Cut along at the seam of the bag and cut off the bottom of the bag so you have a rectangle. Cut the bottom to form a point. Fold down 1 1/2" along one long edge and glue down the end to make a sleeve.

2. Cut a dowel about 2" longer than the width of the banner.

3. Cut a length of yarn about three inches longer than the dowel.

4. Cut four rectangles of the same size from construction paper and roll them into tubes.

5. Glue the tubes on the banner to represent four candles.

6. Draw a flame above each candle.

7. Draw green holly leaves around the base of the candles.

8. Write the words "He Comes" on the banner.

9. Slip the dowel through the sleeve at the top of the banner and tie the yarn to each end.

More to Do

1. Outline or draw flames and leaves with glitter pens or outline with glue and add glitter.

2. Cut the leaves and flames from metallic paper, construction paper, or felt.

3. Write "Hope, Peace, Joy, and Love" on the candles.

4. Roll candles from construction paper using the following color sequence: purple, purple, pink, and purple. (Blue may be used instead of purple.)

5. Cut the bottom of the banner into scallops, points, or fringe. Or glue on tassels or fabric fringes.

6. Decorate the banner with shapes or symbols found elsewhere in this book.

7. Omit the candles and make banners illustrating other seasons and festivals of the church year, as well as other Bible stories or themes.

The Lesson Connection

Advent: Luke 1:68–79

Advent, the four weeks before Christmas, is the time we get ready in our homes and churches for Christmas. Make an Advent banner to remind students of Jesus' coming. As part of your class devotions each week, draw in a flame above a candle. Discuss with students how long God's people waited for the Messiah and that we observe Advent now to celebrate the birth of Jesus, who came to save the world from the darkness of sin, death, and the devil.

Other Lesson Connections

Make banners to illustrate Bible lessons or passages from the Bible.

Use a rolled candle to make a banner illustrating one of the "Lesson Connection" passages for the candle activity on page 16.

Basket

What You Need

Lunch bag
Scissors
Ruler
Pencil
Glue

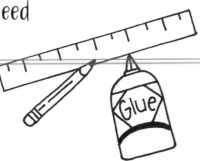

What You Do

1. Measure and mark a horizontal line about 3″ from the top of the paper bag and cut along the line.
2. Fold down the top edge of the bag several times to make a rim.
3. Use a ruler to draw an even number of parallel lines around the sides of the basket. Follow these lines to cut a row of slits around the basket.
4. Cut the top portion of the bag along the seam to make a long rectangle. Use the ruler to draw strips along the length of the rectangle. Cut along these lines.
5. Weave the strips of paper in and out of the slits you have cut into the sides of the basket. Glue the ends where they meet on the inside of the bag. Alternate the in-and-out pattern as you weave other strips of paper.

More to Do

1. Make the basket from a colored paper bag or from a grocery bag.
2. Weave strips of construction paper, tissue paper, ribbon, fabric trim, raffia, or wrapping paper through the basket slits.
3. Cut wavy lines into the basket; cut wavy strips to weave into them.
4. Cut strips and twist them together, then glue them to the inside of the basket to make a handle.
5. To add strength to your basket, cut a second bag so it fits inside the first.
6. Use a marker to write a Bible verse or phrase around the sides or the handle of the basket.
7. Cut shapes or symbols and glue them around the basket. Or put stickers around the basket.
8. Make a basket as a visual aid for a variety of stories or as a prop for a classroom puppet play. Or assemble materials and send them home with students as a take-home craft project.

Other Lesson Connections

Baby Moses in the basket
God sends manna for the children of Israel
The widow's offering
Paul escapes Damascus

The Lesson Connection

Jesus Feeds 5,000: Matthew 14:15–21

When Jesus used a boy's meager meal to feed more than 5,000 people, it was to show His divine power over nature and to teach that He provides for those who believe in Him. Make a basket, then draw and cut out shapes for five loaves and two fishes to put into it. Write "Give Thanks" on the basket as a reminder to give thanks, as Jesus did, for your daily bread.

Beard or Wig

What You Need

Large grocery bag
Markers or crayons
Scissors

What You Do

1. Flatten the bag and draw an oval the same size as a child's forehead, eyes, nose, and mouth—but not the chin. Cut out the face section and the mouth.

2. Color hair and beard. Cut fringe to make bangs and beard. Leave the back and sides as they are, or cut fringe as desired.

3. Put the bag over a child's head as a Bible character mask.

More to Do

1. Use a marker to draw hair or glue on yarn or fabric strips.

2. Before cutting, paint the bag with tempera or craft paint.

3. Change the beard to a mask by cutting out eyeholes only and drawing or painting other facial features.

4. Omit the beard and draw a chin and neck to make a wig for a female Bible character.

5. Have students make beards or wigs for classroom skits or plays for Bible or contemporary lesson applications.

The Lesson Connection

Elijah Is Fed by Ravens: 1 Kings 17:1–6

God cared for Elijah by providing the food he needed. For a lesson review, have a child put on the beard and wig and pretend to be Elijah, sitting by the brook, telling how God sent ravens to bring him food each day. Review the Lord's Prayer, especially "give us this day our daily bread," and discuss the meaning of that petition. Remind children that God provides for all our needs, especially our need for forgiveness of our sins.

Other Lesson Connections

Make beards and wigs to act out Bible stories.

Blocks

What You Need

Medium paper bags
Newspaper
Masking tape

What You Do

1. Crumple newspaper and place it into the bags, then tape the openings closed to form blocks.
2. Stack the blocks to make whatever you need.

More to Do

1. Before stuffing bags, decorate with markers, crayons, or paint. Or cut a brick pattern stamp from foam, apply ink or paint, and stamp onto bags.
2. Make bricks from red bags.
3. Trim the bags to make different shaped blocks.
4. Use blocks to build Bible houses and temples or contemporary houses and churches. Have children make a single block as a craft project, then write an appropriate Bible verse or phrase on it.

Other Lesson Connections

Tower of Babel
The walls of Jericho
Solomon builds the temple
Building the walls of Jerusalem
The house built upon a rock

The Lesson Connection

Christ the Cornerstone: Ephesians 2:19–22

St. Paul called Jesus the "cornerstone," the stone upon which all the other stones in the building depend. He also said that the foundation of God's household is the apostles and prophets. This imagery alludes to the church under construction, meaning it is still growing—through us! Have the children make a "brick" and write on it the words "Built on Christ" as a reminder that Jesus, their Savior, is the cornerstone of their faith. Sing a hymn such as "The Church's One Foundation," "My Hope Is Built on Nothing Less," or "Living Stones."

What You Need

Small paper bag
Masking tape

The Lesson Connection

Jesus Stills a Storm: Mark 4:35–41

The storm was so fierce that Jesus' disciples, seasoned fishermen, were frightened for their lives. Jesus calmed the storm with a few words, and He calmed their fears with His power. Make a boat and several clothespin figures to remind students that Jesus, as true God, has power over the wind and waves of our world too.

Other Lesson Connections

Noah
Jonah
Jesus calls the disciples to be fishers of men
Great catch of fish
Paul's shipwreck

What You Do

1. Fold down the top of the paper bag so you have a section about 1 1/2″ deep.

2. Continue folding to the bottom of the bag.

3. Fold one end of the bag into a point to represent the prow of the boat. Tape the prow.

More to Do

1. Use two paper bags for added strength.

2. Make a sail by cutting a 4″ square of paper. Tape the long end of a bendable straw to the sail, bend the straw and stand it up by taping its short end to the bottom of the boat.

3. Draw faces and clothes on round clothespins. Stick the figures into balls of oil-based clay and stand them inside the boat.

4. Add a piece of vegetable netting to the boat to represent a net.

5. Use markers to add wood grain to the outside of the boat or to add a Bible passage or phrase to the sail.

6. Place the boat on a foam tray with blue construction paper glued inside to represent water.

7. Use your boat as a storytelling aid for a small group or as a take-home craft project.

Book

What You Need

Large paper bag
Scissors
Hole punch
Yarn
Markers or crayons

What You Do

1. Cut down one side of the bag along a crease and cut off the bottom. Cut the large rectangle into equal-sized rectangles.

2. Fold each rectangle in half. Nest the pages together along the fold.

3. Use a hole punch to make two holes on the center fold.

4. Thread a piece of yarn through the holes and tie a bow along the spine of the book.

5. Use markers or crayons to write and illustrate the book.

More to Do

1. Use small paper bags to make a photo album. In the corners of each page, draw pictures to illustrate Bible stories or write Bible verses along the bottom of the pages.

2. Use a variety of colored bags for pages.

3. Decorate the book with scrapbook materials or pictures from newspapers, magazines, or the Internet.

4. Tear pieces from a paper bag or magazine and glue them over the cover sheet.

5. Make books to use in teaching Bible stories. Have students make books to use in telling the story to someone else or in applying the story to their lives.

The Lesson Connection

Timothy: 2 Timothy 1:3–10

When Timothy was a boy, his mother and grandmother taught him Bible stories. When he grew up, Timothy studied under Peter and preached the Gospel. In other words, Timothy served the early Christian church as a pastor. Have the children make a scrapbook that includes their favorite Bible stories and photos of their families, their classmates, and themselves. Remind them that in everything we do, we are God's baptized and redeemed children.

Other Lesson Connections

Make a book illustrating a favorite psalm.

Luke writes about Jesus; write a book to tell someone else about Jesus.

Write a story that applies a Bible lesson to the student's life, such as Jesus' baptism and our Baptism into Christ.

Bottle Puppet

What You Need

Lunch bag
Chenille stick
Plastic bottle
Newspaper
Scissors
Rubber band
Glue
Markers
Yarn (optional)

What You Do

1. Wrap newspaper around a chenille stick, then wrap the chenille stick around the neck of the bottle to create arms.

2. To make the bag easier to work with, crumple the bag and flatten it again before stuffing the face.

3. Wad a piece of newspaper into a ball and fit it into the bottom of the bag.

4. Fit the bag over the bottle and slip a rubber band around it at the character's neck to hold it in place.

5. Cut slits into each side of the bag and slip the chenille stick arms through the holes. Glue in place.

6. Use markers to add facial features, hair, and clothing to the figure. Or glue lengths of yarn onto the head for hair.

More to Do

1. Use bags in a variety of colors, or decorate puppets with construction paper, colored tissue, fabric, yarn, or fabric trim.

2. Omit the chenille stick arms and draw arms onto the bag, or roll paper and glue on for arms.

3. Trim the sides of the bag and glue the paper directly to the side of the bottle.

4. Glue movable craft eyes to the puppet face.

5. Use optional face patterns found on pages 59—63 to make teaching puppets.

6. Instead of people, make animal bottle figures.

7. Vary bottle sizes for characters of different sizes.

8. Make bottle puppets as simple classroom storytelling aids or as take-home crafts.

The Lesson Connection

Lydia: Acts 16:11–15

Lydia was a businesswoman in Philippi who heard Paul tell of Jesus. She sold purple cloth, which was a luxury item in Bible times. God opened Lydia's heart to believe in Jesus as her Savior and she and her household were baptized into Christ. Make a puppet to represent Lydia. Explain to students that faith is a gift of God to us at our Baptism.

Other Lesson Connections

Noah's Ark
David and Goliath
Jesus' birth
Easter

Candle

What You Need

Lunch bag
Markers or crayons
Scissors
Newspaper
Glue stick

What You Do

1. Place the bag flat on the table. Draw a candle shape on one side of the bag. The top of the bag is the flame of the candle. Optional pattern on page 58.
2. Cut out the candle shape, making sure to cut through all layers of the bag at the same time.
3. Color the candle and the flame.
4. Write a Bible verse or phrase on the candle.
5. Stuff the bag with newspaper, then glue the top edges of the bag together.

More to Do

1. Cut the candle from a decorative gift bag or cover the front and back with wrapping paper or construction paper.
2. Cut the flame from construction paper or metallic gift wrap.
3. Embellish the flame with glitter, glitter glue, or sequins.
4. Write a Bible passage, phrase, or hymn on the candle, or draw a cross on a white candle to make it a "Christ candle."

The Lesson Connection

Song of Simeon: Luke 2:21–35

Simeon took Jesus in his arms and praised God for sending this little baby—God in the flesh—to be a "light for all people." Make a candle and write, "Jesus is my Light" on it. Have students join you in a prayer thanking God for sending Jesus to light the way to heaven through His life, sacrificial death, and resurrection from the grave.

Other Lesson Connections

"The Lord is my light and my salvation." Psalm 27:1

"Arise, shine, for your light has come." Isaiah 60:1

Jesus said, "I am the light of the world." John 8:12

Song prop for "This Little Gospel Light of Mine"

Card

What You Need

Lunch bag
Scissors
Ruler
Pencil
Markers or crayons

What You Do

1. Cut along the seam of the bag then cut off the bottom to make a long rectangle.

2. Use a ruler to measure and mark a rectangle to the desired size. Cut away excess paper.

3. Fold the card and decorate it.

More to Do

1. Use glitter paint, fabric paint, construction paper, fabric, sequins, ribbon, raffia, stickers, or fabric trim to decorate the card.

2. Stamp designs on the card or use paint and a stencil.

3. Use different colors and sizes of bags. Cut paper with scrapbook scissors.

4. Trace a cookie cutter design on the card and sew around it with yarn.

5. Copy and trace one of the patterns on pages 56 and 58.

6. Glue construction or computer paper inside the card and write a greeting, Bible verse, or blessing.

7. Make cards to give others as part of a lesson application.

The Lesson Connection

Christmas: Luke 2:1–20

After the shepherds saw baby Jesus, they rushed to spread the news of the Messiah's birth among all they met. Discuss with students why this was such Good News, that the long-awaited Old Testament prophecies about the Savior had been fulfilled in Bethlehem through the birth of this baby. Make a Christmas card to share with someone else your joy that Jesus came to save us from all our sin and to bring us forgiveness and eternal life.

Other Lesson Connections

Jesus heals a little girl (Make a get-well card.)

Jesus' baptism (Make a birthday or a Baptism birthday card.)

Easter

Cornucopia

What You Need
Small paper bag

What You Do
1. Fold back the top edge of the bag 1″. Fold back again to make a rim.
2. Beginning at the bottom of the bag, twist it all the way to the top. Open the top of the bag to make a circle.
3. Fill the bag with objects that reflect the lesson theme.

More to Do
1. Write an appropriate Bible verse or phrase onto the bag.
2. Make papier mâché fruit to place in the cornucopia: Mix flour and water to make a paste. Tear a paper bag into strips and dip them into the paste. Wrap strips around crumpled newspaper until you have formed it into fruit shapes. Let dry completely, then paint with tempera or acrylic paint.
3. Use the cornucopia as a teaching aid: Fill it with pictures or miniatures of things for which we give thanks to God.
4. Make a cornucopia from a large grocery bag to use as a mission project: Fill it with items to give to others in need, such as school supplies for an inner city school

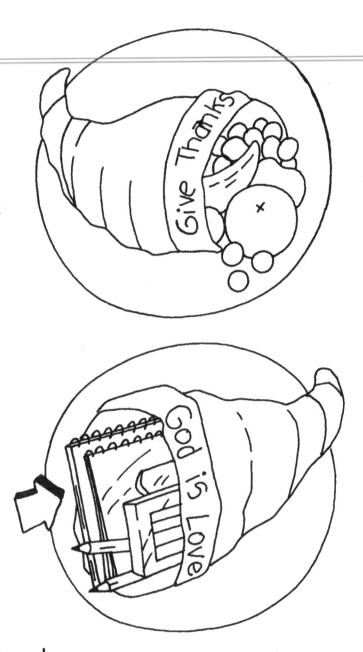

The Lesson Connection

Jesus Heals Ten Lepers: Luke 17:11–19

Jesus healed ten lepers, but only one of them returned to thank Him. This Bible story is often used in Thanksgiving church services as a model for us to follow in giving thanks. Jesus healed the leper of his disease, and He heals us of the disease called sin. Make a classroom cornucopia and have each student draw a picture of something for which they are thankful to put into it. Pull the pictures out one-by-one as you lead the children in a classroom prayer of thanksgiving. Sing "Now Thank We All Our God" or another appropriate hymn.

Other Lesson Connections

"Give thanks to the LORD." Psalm 136:1
Jesus gave thanks before He distributed the bread and wine at the Last Supper.
The early Christians

Cross

What You Need

Lunch bag
Scissors
Pencil
White glue
Water
Brush
Hole punch
Yarn or ribbon

What You Do

1. Cut a paper bag along the seam and cut off the bottom so you have a rectangle.

2. Flatten the rectangle and cut three or more identical crosses. (Optional pattern on page 56.)

3. Make a mixture of equal parts white glue and water. Use it to glue the crosses together and to brush over the top of the cross when finished. Allow glue to dry completely.

4. Punch a hole in the top of the cross, thread yarn or ribbon through the hole, and hang.

The Lesson Connection

Good Friday: John 19:17–37

Although the students in your classroom will already know the cross as a symbol for Jesus, some may not understand that it is an expression of forgiveness and glory. Make a Good Friday cross from a brown paper bag to help you teach children that Jesus died to take away the world's sins and to bring salvation to repentant believers. Twist a strip of paper and glue it in a circle to represent the crown of thorns soldiers put upon Jesus. Then glue it to the cross. Lead children in a song such as "Glory Be to Jesus" or "Do You Know Who Died for Me?"

Other Lesson Connections

"God so loved the world." John 3:16
(Glue a paper heart to the center of the cross.)
Easter (empty cross)
Galatians 3:13–14

More to Do

1. Cut a strip of paper, twist it, then glue the ends to make a "crown of thorns." Glue it to the center of the cross.

2. Options for decorating include stickers, fabric pieces, construction paper, gift-wrap, tissue paper, yarn, dried flowers, or fabric trim.

3. Glue the crosses together using a glue stick. Omit the water-and-glue mixture. Use markers or crayons to draw wood-grain lines or to write a Bible passage or phrase.

4. Use raffia, twine, or other craft material as a hanger.

5. Instead of cutting out individual crosses, first glue several pieces of paper together, trace a cross shape, then cut it out. Or cut two strips of paper and glue them together at a right angle to make a cross.

6. Make the cross from a colored paper bag.

7. Make a plaque: Use one of the other shapes or symbols in this book as a base, make the cross described here, glue the cross to the base, and hang the plaque in the classroom.

8. Use a grocery bag to make a large classroom cross or have children make smaller crosses to take home.

Cross Basket

What You Need

Paper bag
Scissors
Ruler
Pencil
Glue
Markers or crayons

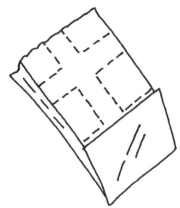

What You Do

1. Lay the bag with the bottom flap facing up.
2. Use a ruler to outline a cross. The top and sides of the cross should extend to the top and sides of the bag, and the bottom of the cross should meet the edge of the flap. (Optional: Use cross pattern on page 56.)
3. Cut away the bag so the cross shape stays intact at the sides and bottom, as shown.
4. Glue the top edges of the crosses together for a handle.
5. Decorate and fill the basket as you wish.

More to Do

1. Nest another bag inside the first and cut a cross on only one side of one bag.
2. Fill the bag with items that illustrate the lesson you are teaching. Pull out the items as you tell the story.
3. Decorate the bag with stickers, markers, crayons, construction paper, tissue paper, or other craft materials.
4. Use as a classroom storytelling aid or as a gift bag.

The Lesson Connection

Easter: Luke 24:1–12

An Alleluia basket is a fun way to celebrate the joy you have in knowing that Jesus died and rose for you! Make the cross from a colored paper bag and decorate it with religious Easter stickers. Fill with Easter grass and candy, such as jellybeans in colors that symbolize the events of Jesus' death and resurrection.

Other Lesson Connections

Good Friday storytelling bag (Place in the bag items representing Jesus' death.)
Easter storytelling bag (Place in the bag items representing Jesus' resurrection.)

Crown

A Crown of Life

What You Need

Medium paper bag
Scissors
Pencil

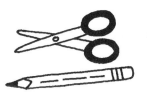

What You Do

1. Cut off the bottom of the bag so you have a ring.
2. Roll the bottom edge of the ring several times to make a rim.
3. Trim off the excess. Cut a row of zigzag triangles along the top as shown here.
4. If needed, size the crown to the head of the person wearing it.

More to Do

1. Cut other styles of crowns using different cuts along the top.
2. Add fabric trim, construction paper, tissue paper, or sequins. Or paint the crown with glue and sprinkle glitter over the glue before it dries.
3. Make a small crown from a lunch bag and write a Bible verse or phrase on it.
4. Use a colored paper bag to make the crown.
5. Make crowns to use as costumes for one of the many Bible stories in which there is a king.

Other Lesson Connections

David
Solomon
Esther
Wise Men
Revelation 15:3–4

The Lesson Connection

Crown of Life: Revelation 2:10

On Christ the King Sunday, the last Sunday in the church year, we celebrate Jesus as the King of heaven. As true God, Jesus is the Lord of all! Make a crown and write around it the words "Jesus is my King." Decorate the crown with sequins and glitter glue.

Diorama

What You Need

Paper bag
Pencil
Scissors
Construction paper
Markers or crayons
Glue

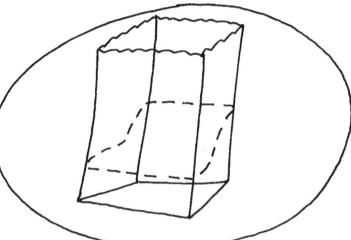

What You Do

1. Cut the bag as shown in the drawing. Then flatten the bag and draw the outline of an appropriate background (grass, trees, hills, buildings, etc.) inside and outside to create the setting of the diorama. Cut out and color your outline. Fringe grass if desired.

2. On construction paper, draw figures and shapes (such as trees and boulders) to go inside the background. Cut out each figure with a ½″ tab at the bottom. (See pattern ideas on page 57.) Stand figures and shapes by folding the tab and gluing it down.

More to Do

1. Glue tissue, fabric, or other craft materials onto the diorama.

2. Write a Bible passage or motto around the bag.

3. Make the diorama from a colored paper bag.

4. Make dioramas to use in teaching a Bible lesson to a small group. Or have students make them to take home and tell the lesson to someone else.

The Lesson Connection

Jesus in Gethsemane: Matthew 26:36–46

"May Your will be done," Jesus prayed to His heavenly Father in the Garden of Gethsemane. Have each child make a diorama from a lunch bag. Add shapes representing Jesus kneeling in prayer beside a rock. As the children work, talk about how Jesus knew that His death was necessary to fulfill God's plan for our salvation. Jesus loves us so much He willingly died on the cross for our sins. If the children in your class are very young, sing a song like "Jesus Loves Me"; with older students, sing a hymn, such as "Go to Dark Gethsemane."

Other Lesson Connections

Creation
Noah's Ark
The fiery furnace
Christmas
Jesus' baptism

Dove

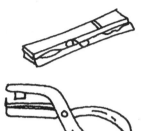

What You Need

White lunch bag
Scissors
Newspaper
Glue
Clothespin
Markers or crayons
Hole punch
White yarn

What You Do

1. Photocopy the patterns on page 58 and trace them onto one side of a white bag. Trace the cloud on the bottom portion of the bag and the dove's beak pointing toward the open end.

2. Cut out the dove shape, cutting both sides of the bag at the same time and leaving it attached to the cloud-shaped bag bottom.

3. Glue the doves together, leaving a hole for stuffing. When the glue is dry, stuff with crumpled newspaper and glue the hole shut. If necessary, use the clothespin to hold the bag shut until the glue dries.

4. Use markers or crayons to add eyes and a beak to the dove.

5. Use a hole punch to make two holes in the bottom of the bag.

6. Cut a length of yarn and tie it through the holes for a hanger.

The Lesson Connection

Jesus' Baptism: Matthew 3:11–17

When Jesus was baptized, the Holy Spirit came down like a dove and God the Father spoke from heaven, saying, "This is My Son, whom I love." Make a dove mobile to teach students that on the day of their Baptism, the Holy Spirit gave them the gift of faith. Through the water and the Word, their sins were washed away and God adopted them as His own dear children. Have each child make a dove and write his name and baptismal date on the cloud.

More to Do

1. Write appropriate words or a Bible verse on the cloud part of the bag.

2. Use glitter, glitter glue, construction paper, fabric, or fabric trim to add details to the cloud and dove.

3. Glue cotton balls to the cloud and feathers to the dove.

4. Cut a leaf from green construction paper and glue it to the beak to make a "dove of peace."

5. Use the dove for a storytelling prop, a classroom decoration, or a take-home craft project.

Other Lesson Connections

Noah's Ark
Pentecost

23

Finger Puppet Stage

What You Need

Lunch bag
Scissors
Markers or crayons
Water-based, fine-tipped markers

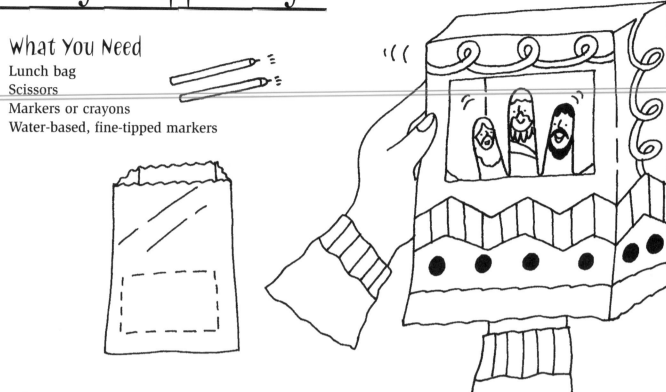

What You Do

1. Open the bag and cut a rectangle near the bottom of one side as shown.

2. Flatten the bag and decorate both the outside and inside to make the stage background.

3. Use fine-tipped markers to draw faces on your fingertips.

4. Hold the bag stage with your free hand and act out a story with finger-tip puppets.

More to Do

1. Paint the theater with tempera paint or glue on fabric, construction paper, stickers, or fabric trim.

2. Glue a picture inside the bag for a stage backdrop.

3. Instead of drawing on your fingertips, make finger puppets from paper. Draw story characters on strips of paper sized to fit your fingers, glue the edges together to make cylinders, and slip them over your fingers. (See patterns on page 57.)

4. Use the "finger-tip theatre" for a lesson presentation in a small group setting or as a classroom craft for each child to take home.

The Lesson Connection

Transfiguration: Mark 9:2–13

Moses and Elijah appeared with Jesus on a high mountain, and the voice of God came from heaven saying, "This is My beloved Son." Use a washable marker to draw three finger puppets to use in telling the story to your class. Explain that at His Transfiguration, Jesus appeared with the Old Testament prophets to show that He was the fulfillment of the prophecies to Israel—He is the promised Messiah. God's voice from the cloud was proof that He is God's true Son.

Other Lesson Connections

Use puppets to represent any Bible story.

Use puppets to represent contemporary children for lesson applications.

Flower

What You Need
Colored paper bags (2)
Scissors
Green chenille stick
Floral tape
Glue (optional)

More to Do

1. Fringe or cut scallops along the flower side of the bag.

2. Use a rubber band to attach the flower to a dowel.

3. Write an appropriate Bible verse or phrase on the outside of the flower or on a small card attached to it.

4. Tie decorative ribbons to the base of the flower.

5. Add construction or tissue paper leaves to the base of the flower.

6. Fold over another bag, decorate the outside, and use it as a vase for the flower.

7. Color a white paper bag to make a rainbow-colored flower.

8. Make the flower from only one paper bag.

9. Make smaller flowers from different colored paper bags.

What You Do

1. Cut off the bottoms of two paper bags.

2. Twist the bottom of one bag.

3. Fit the twisted end of the first bag inside the second, slip in the end of a green chenille stick, and twist the end of the outside bag.

4. Cut and wrap floral tape around the twisted bag ends to fasten them to the chenille stick. Optional: Glue the twisted ends to the chenille stick.

The Lesson Connection

God Cares for the Bird and Flowers: Luke 12:22–34

Jesus once reminded His friends that God, who takes care of the beautiful flowers, also takes care of all our needs—especially our need for forgiveness for our sins. Make a flower to remind you of this. Use a fine-tipped marker to write "God cares for (name)" onto the flower. Use this craft and lesson connection to help children come to terms with their fears. Sing a song or hymn, such as "God Loves Me Dearly" or "I Am Trusting You, Lord Jesus."

Other Lesson Connections

Creation
"I am a rose of Sharon, a lily of the valleys."
Song of Solomon 2:1
Easter (Make a classroom Easter garden.)

Gift Bag

What You Need

Paper bag
Hole punch
Yarn
Tape
Markers, crayons, or stickers
Tissue paper

What You Do

1. Fold the top of the bag to the inside about 1 1/2".

2. Punch two sets of holes through the folded paper on opposite sides of the bag.

3. Cut two lengths of yarn. To make handles, thread yarn through the holes on each side and tape the ends to the inside of the bag.

4. Fold the bag flat in front of you and decorate it with markers, crayons, or stickers.

5. Add tissue paper and a gift to the inside of the bag.

More to Do

1. Decorate the bag with photos, paper shapes, paint, or fabric trim.

2. Write an appropriate Bible verse or phrase on the bag.

3. Make a gift bag as an application for Bible stories about the love God has for us and wants us to show to one another.

4. Use shapes and symbols found elsewhere in this book. (See patterns on pages 56 and 58.)

5. Make gift bags from a variety of colored bags.

The Lesson Connection

Dorcas: Acts 9:36–42

Dorcas responded to God's love by showing love to others—she made clothing for them. When Dorcas became sick and died, God sent Peter to make her alive again. Make a gift bag to fill with a gift for someone else. Decorate it with hearts cut from paper. Write "God loves you" on the bag.

Other Lesson Connections

David helps Jonathan's son
Good Samaritan
"Freely you have received, freely give." Matthew 10:8

Flower

What You Need

Colored paper bags (2)
Scissors
Green chenille stick
Floral tape
Glue (optional)

More to Do

1. Fringe or cut scallops along the flower side of the bag.

2. Use a rubber band to attach the flower to a dowel.

3. Write an appropriate Bible verse or phrase on the outside of the flower or on a small card attached to it.

4. Tie decorative ribbons to the base of the flower.

5. Add construction or tissue paper leaves to the base of the flower.

6. Fold over another bag, decorate the outside, and use it as a vase for the flower.

7. Color a white paper bag to make a rainbow-colored flower.

8. Make the flower from only one paper bag.

9. Make smaller flowers from different colored paper bags.

What You Do

1. Cut off the bottoms of two paper bags.

2. Twist the bottom of one bag.

3. Fit the twisted end of the first bag inside the second, slip in the end of a green chenille stick, and twist the end of the outside bag.

4. Cut and wrap floral tape around the twisted bag ends to fasten them to the chenille stick. Optional: Glue the twisted ends to the chenille stick.

The Lesson Connection

God Cares for the Bird and Flowers: Luke 12:22–34

Jesus once reminded His friends that God, who takes care of the beautiful flowers, also takes care of all our needs—especially our need for forgiveness for our sins. Make a flower to remind you of this. Use a fine-tipped marker to write "God cares for (name)" onto the flower. Use this craft and lesson connection to help children come to terms with their fears. Sing a song or hymn, such as "God Loves Me Dearly" or "I Am Trusting You, Lord Jesus."

Other Lesson Connections

Creation
"I am a rose of Sharon, a lily of the valleys."
Song of Solomon 2:1
Easter (Make a classroom Easter garden.)

25

Gift Bag

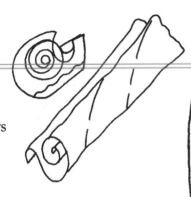

What You Need

Paper bag
Hole punch
Yarn
Tape
Markers, crayons, or stickers
Tissue paper

What You Do

1. Fold the top of the bag to the inside about 1 ½".

2. Punch two sets of holes through the folded paper on opposite sides of the bag.

3. Cut two lengths of yarn. To make handles, thread yarn through the holes on each side and tape the ends to the inside of the bag.

4. Fold the bag flat in front of you and decorate it with markers, crayons, or stickers.

5. Add tissue paper and a gift to the inside of the bag.

More to Do

1. Decorate the bag with photos, paper shapes, paint, or fabric trim.

2. Write an appropriate Bible verse or phrase on the bag.

3. Make a gift bag as an application for Bible stories about the love God has for us and wants us to show to one another.

4. Use shapes and symbols found elsewhere in this book. (See patterns on pages 56 and 58.)

5. Make gift bags from a variety of colored bags.

The Lesson Connection

Dorcas: Acts 9:36–42

Dorcas responded to God's love by showing love to others—she made clothing for them. When Dorcas became sick and died, God sent Peter to make her alive again. Make a gift bag to fill with a gift for someone else. Decorate it with hearts cut from paper. Write "God loves you" on the bag.

Other Lesson Connections

David helps Jonathan's son
Good Samaritan
"Freely you have received, freely give." Matthew 10:8

Hand Puppet

(Movable Flap)

What You Need

Lunch bag
Markers
Scissors

What You Do

1. Place a flat paper bag in front of you with the bottom facing up.

2. On the bottom, draw or glue on a nose, two eyes, and the top of a mouth. On the bag below the fold, draw or glue on the bottom of a mouth.

3. Use markers to add hair, a beard, and a robe.

More to Do

1. Draw a face on a piece of paper, color it, and cut it out. Cut across the face at the mouth. Glue the top part of the face on the bottom of the bag, aligning it on the fold. Glue the bottom part of the face on the bag below the fold.

2. Make the face from different pieces of construction paper. Cut and glue on construction paper or fabric for the robe.

3. Use one of the patterns at the back of the book to make faces from construction paper.

4. Make animal hand puppets (patterns found at the back of the book).

5. Make puppets from different colored paper bags.

6. Use curling ribbon, yarn, or craft hair for puppet hair. Or cut strips of construction paper and curl them around a pencil or along the edge of a dull plastic knife.

7. Make a set of puppets to use in telling a variety of Bible stories. Have children make puppets for specific stories to take home and share with others.

The Lesson Connection

Mary and Martha: Luke 10:38–42

While Martha was busy preparing the meal for their important guest, Mary sat at Jesus' feet, listening and learning from what He said. Martha's work was important but Mary's action shows where our priority should be—Jesus' words to us. Make hand puppets to use to tell the story to the class. When done, talk with students about where we learn more about God's Word for us.

Other Lesson Connections

Sampson
Daniel in the lions' den
Jesus, the Good Shepherd, and lambs
Wise Men and camels
Use puppets to represent contemporary children for lesson applications.

Hand Puppet

(Stuffed Head)

What You Need

Lunch bag
Markers or crayons
Newspaper
Rubber band
Scissors

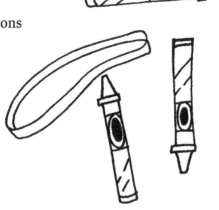

What You Do

1. Flatten the bag and place it in front of you with the flap down. Draw a face on the top half of the bag.

2. Crumple a piece of newspaper and fit it into the top of the bag. Gather the bag at the neck and slip a rubber band over it, leaving enough room for you to slip a finger through.

3. Cut a slit at each side of the puppet body.

4. Fit your hand inside the puppet with the index finger inside the head and the thumb and little finger sticking through the slits for arms.

More to Do

1. Reinforce the finger slits by gluing two bags together or by gluing a second layer of paper on the inside of the bag at the point where you are going to cut.

2. Use bags in a variety of colors to make the puppets, or decorate them with construction paper, colored tissue, fabric, or fabric trim.

3. Glue movable craft eyes on the puppet face.

4. Duplicate, color, and glue on one of the face patterns found at the end of this book.

5. Make a set of teaching puppets, or have children make puppets to use in telling the lesson to someone else or for a lesson application.

The Lesson Connection

The Jailer at Philippi: Acts 16:16–34

"What must I do to be saved?" asked the jailer at Philippi. "Believe in the Lord Jesus Christ and you will be saved," answered Paul. Paul and Silas had been beaten and imprisoned, but they continued to witness to their faith in the Lord God. Their faith and a powerful earthquake got the jailer's attention. The jailer and the others in his house came to faith through the Word of God and were baptized. Make puppets for Paul, Silas, and the jailer to use in teaching this story.

Other Lesson Connections

Use puppets to represent Bible characters.

Use puppets to represent contemporary children for lesson applications.

Hanging Ornament

What You Need

Paper bag
Cookie cutters
Pencil
Fabric
Pinking shears
Glue
Hole punch
Raffia

What You Do

1. Use cookie cutters as patterns to trace shapes on the fabric. Cut out shapes with pinking shears.
2. Cut along the seam of the paper bag and cut off the bottom to make a rectangular sheet of paper.
3. Glue shapes to the paper bag and cut them out with the pinking sheers, leaving a 1/2" around the fabric.
4. Punch a hole at the top of the ornament and tie a piece of raffia through it for hanging.

More to Do

1. Glue rickrack, yarn, buttons, or other trim around the shape. Decorate the ornament with glitter glue or textured fabric paint.
2. Use regular scissors instead of pinking shears.
3. Instead of fabric, use wallpaper, wrapping paper, or construction paper.
4. For more stability, glue several layers of shapes together.
5. Instead of cookie cutter patterns, choose patterns on pages 56 and 58 or elsewhere in this book.
6. Make stuffed ornaments: Cut two identical shapes, line the edges with glue—leaving space for stuffing—and glue the two shapes together. Stuff with a cotton ball or facial tissue then glue the opening.
7. Use yarn or ribbon instead of raffia.
8. Make ornaments to use on mobiles to decorate your classroom or as a craft to take home.

The Lesson Connection

Christmas: Luke 2

"Joy to the world," we sing at Christmas, "the Lord has come!" Have children celebrate their joy that Jesus came to earth to be their Lord and Savior by making Christmas ornaments to put on the classroom Christmas tree or to give a special friend.

Other Lesson Connections

Lent and Easter (cross)
Epiphany (star)
Pentecost (tongues of fire)
God's love (heart)

29

Hat

What You Need
Grocery bag
Scissors
Fabric trim
Glue

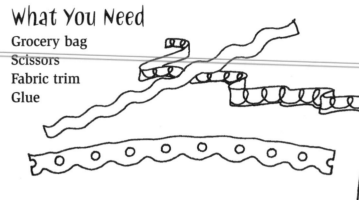

What You Do

1. Cut paper bag in half, then roll the cut edge up several times to form a brim.
2. Glue on decorative fabric trim.
3. Fit the hat to your head, fold over the excess, then staple.

More to Do

1. Paint the hat with tempera paint.
2. Use markers to decorate the hat.
3. Add stickers or adhesive plastic gems.
4. Glue on pieces of fabric, colored tissue, or wrapping paper.

The Lesson Connection

The Wise Men: Matthew 2:1–12

Well aware of Jewish prophecies and traditions, Wise Men from the East followed a star to find the baby King so they could worship Him and honor Him with gifts. Have students make turban-like hats to wear as they pretend to be the Magi, acting out the story of the search for the King and their joy at finding Him at last. Sing a carol like "We Three Kings" or an Epiphany hymn like "As with Gladness Men of Old" and explain that, like the Wise Men, we also go to worship the King.

Other Lesson Connections

Create hats representing the costumes of various ethnic groups. Wear them as you talk about God's love for all people.

Hanging Ornament

What You Need

Paper bag
Cookie cutters
Pencil
Fabric
Pinking shears
Glue
Hole punch
Raffia

What You Do

1. Use cookie cutters as patterns to trace shapes on the fabric. Cut out shapes with pinking shears.
2. Cut along the seam of the paper bag and cut off the bottom to make a rectangular sheet of paper.
3. Glue shapes to the paper bag and cut them out with the pinking sheers, leaving a 1/2″ around the fabric.
4. Punch a hole at the top of the ornament and tie a piece of raffia through it for hanging.

More to Do

1. Glue rickrack, yarn, buttons, or other trim around the shape. Decorate the ornament with glitter glue or textured fabric paint.
2. Use regular scissors instead of pinking shears.
3. Instead of fabric, use wallpaper, wrapping paper, or construction paper.
4. For more stability, glue several layers of shapes together.
5. Instead of cookie cutter patterns, choose patterns on pages 56 and 58 or elsewhere in this book.
6. Make stuffed ornaments: Cut two identical shapes, line the edges with glue—leaving space for stuffing—and glue the two shapes together. Stuff with a cotton ball or facial tissue then glue the opening.
7. Use yarn or ribbon instead of raffia.
8. Make ornaments to use on mobiles to decorate your classroom or as a craft to take home.

The Lesson Connection

Christmas: Luke 2

"Joy to the world," we sing at Christmas, "the Lord has come!" Have children celebrate their joy that Jesus came to earth to be their Lord and Savior by making Christmas ornaments to put on the classroom Christmas tree or to give a special friend.

Other Lesson Connections

Lent and Easter (cross)
Epiphany (star)
Pentecost (tongues of fire)
God's love (heart)

Hat

What You Need

Grocery bag
Scissors
Fabric trim
Glue

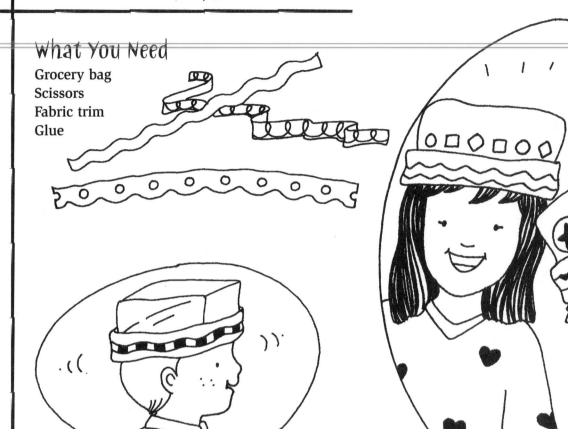

What You Do

1. Cut paper bag in half, then roll the cut edge up several times to form a brim.
2. Glue on decorative fabric trim.
3. Fit the hat to your head, fold over the excess, then staple.

More to Do

1. Paint the hat with tempera paint.
2. Use markers to decorate the hat.
3. Add stickers or adhesive plastic gems.
4. Glue on pieces of fabric, colored tissue, or wrapping paper.

The Lesson Connection

The Wise Men: Matthew 2:1–12

Well aware of Jewish prophecies and traditions, Wise Men from the East followed a star to find the baby King so they could worship Him and honor Him with gifts. Have students make turban-like hats to wear as they pretend to be the Magi, acting out the story of the search for the King and their joy at finding Him at last. Sing a carol like "We Three Kings" or an Epiphany hymn like "As with Gladness Men of Old" and explain that, like the Wise Men, we also go to worship the King.

Other Lesson Connections

Create hats representing the costumes of various ethnic groups. Wear them as you talk about God's love for all people.

Helmet

What You Need

Medium paper bag
Pencil
Scissors
Markers or paper and glue

The Lesson Connection

**Jesus Heals the Centurion's Servant:
Luke 7:1–10**

"My servant is sick," the soldier said to Jesus, "please heal him." Jesus called attention to the Roman soldier's faith and healed the servant instantly. Make a helmet for a child to wear as he or she pretends to be the soldier retelling the story. Explain that Jesus cured the servant's illness, and He heals the illness of our sin through His forgiveness, providing eternal life to those who would repent and believe.

Other Lesson Connections

David and Goliath
Good Friday
"Helmet of salvation." Ephesians 6:17

What You Do

1. Trace a helmet shape onto the bag. (See pattern on page 64.) Cut out the remaining area as shown.

2. Decorate with markers or paper.

More to Do

1. Cut out the helmet according to the diagrams found on this page. Cut out and glue on additional pieces as desired.

2. Decorate helmet with paint, glitter glue, sequins, construction paper, yarn, felt, or fabric trim.

3. Write a Bible passage or phrase on the helmet.

4. Make helmets as props to use in storytelling or as take-home crafts to illustrate a specific Bible verse.

House

What You Need

Paper bag
Markers or crayons
Newspaper
Glue
Construction paper
Scissors

What You Do

1. Lay the flat paper bag in front of you and draw the windows and door of a house.

2. Stuff the bottom half of the bag with newspaper.

3. Glue the top of the bag together and fold it to form the roof of the house.

4. Cut a construction paper rectangle as the roof and glue in place.

More to Do

1. Make a church instead of a house.

2. Paint the house with tempera paint.

3. Omit the construction paper roof and draw shingles or thatch.

4. Write a Bible passage on the roof or front of the house.

5. Draw windows and doors for the rest of the house.

6. Draw members of your family looking out of the doors and windows.

7. Glue a photograph of yourself in one of the windows or inside the door.

8. Make houses for a classroom activity center or have children make a house to take home as a lesson application.

The Lesson Connection

Joshua's Farewell Speech: Joshua 24:15

"As for me and my house," Joshua said, "we will serve the Lord." Joshua was strongly urging the children of Israel to stop worshiping false gods and turn toward the one true God, but his words are just as appropriate in our time. People today may be distracted by a variety of "gods": sports, television, career, and the like. But we should fear and love God above all else. Have children make a house representing their own home. Write "God Bless Our Home" on the roof as a reminder to stay true to the first commandment.

Other Lesson Connections

Solomon's temple (Make a church.)
The house built upon a rock

Map

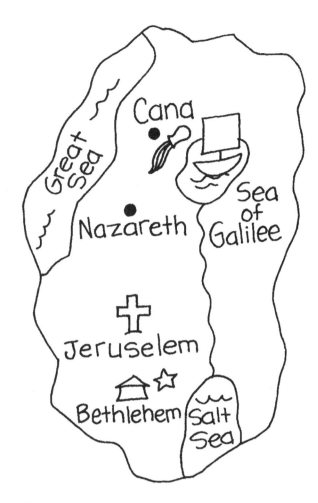

Cana

Great Sea

Nazareth

Sea of Galilee

Jeruselem

Bethlehem Salt Sea

What You Need

Brown paper bag
Markers

The Lesson Connection

Jesus' Ministry: Matthew, Mark, Luke, John

During the Son of God's three years of ministry on earth, He traveled from town to town, healing, teaching, and forgiving the sins of the people. Make a map that shows key places Jesus visited. Have the children draw pictures on the map to illustrate events that happened at these places, particularly how His journeys led to His crucifixion and resurrection. As the children work, explain that Jesus was a real, historical figure and that in the Holy Land today the ruins of the places He visited can still be seen.

What You Do

1. Tear a rectangle shape from the paper bag.
2. Crumple the rectangle and spread it out again.
3. Draw a map on the paper.
4. Use a dark brown marker to outline the torn edge of the paper.

More to Do

1. Use tempera paint, watercolor, or colored pencils to add other details to the map.
2. Write an appropriate Bible verse or phrase onto the map.
3. Omit the torn outline and place the map on a table for a tabletop stage. Move wooden craft figures or small puppets over the map as you tell Bible stories.
4. Make a large map illustrating a specific story or series of stories. Or, for a lesson application, have children make a map of places they go where Jesus is with them.

Other Lesson Connections

Abraham and Sarah
Jacob
Joseph
Children of Israel in the wilderness
Paul's missionary journeys

33

Mask

Jesus Saves!

What You Need

Large paper bag
Markers or crayons
Scissors

What You Do

1. Flatten a large paper bag on the work surface in front of you.
2. Draw a face on the bag.
3. Cut holes for eyes and mouth.
4. Trim the bag as needed to make hair and a beard.
5. Put the bag over your head to wear it.

More to Do

1. Glue on fabric, yarn, construction paper, and other fabric trim to add details to the mask.
2. Make masks of Bible animals.
3. Make a set of masks to use for a variety of classroom Bible stories.

The Lesson Connection

Paul: Acts 9:1–31

Saul traveled to Damascus with a single-minded purpose—to persecute the Christians there. But God had other plans for him. The resurrected Jesus appeared to Saul. He was brought to faith and was baptized. He spent the rest of his life telling others about Jesus and His love. Draw an "angry Saul" on one side of the mask and a "happy Paul" on the other. Turn the mask around as you tell the story.

Other Lesson Connections

Creation (Make masks representing animals made by God.)

Make masks to represent all of the characters in a particular Bible story.

Make masks to represent contemporary children for lesson applications.

34

Mobile

The Lesson Connection

Miriam's Song of Praise: Exodus 15:1–21

After the children of Israel crossed the Red Sea on the safe, dry path God made for them, Miriam sang a song of praise for their salvation: "Sing to the LORD, for He is highly exalted." Have the students make a "praise mobile" to remind them to praise God each day for delivering them from their enemies (sin, death, devil). Cut circles into the side of the bag. Draw or glue on shapes for musical notes and write, "Praise the Lord" on the sides of the bag. Decorate with bright streamers.

Other Lesson Connections
Jacob's ladder
Christmas (angels or stars)
Trinity (triangles)

What You Need
Paper bag (any size or color)
Scissors
Construction or tissue paper
Glue
Marker
Hole punch
Yarn

What You Do

1. Place the flattened bag on the table with the opening facing toward you.

2. Cut symmetrical designs (triangles, circles, hearts, etc.) along the side folds of the bag.

3. Write an appropriate Bible verse or phrase on the bag.

4. Cut strips of tissue paper or construction paper and glue them along the inside bottom of the bag. Cut decorative shapes and glue them around the outside of the bag. (See patterns on pages 56 and 58.)

5. Punch holes at the top and tie a piece of yarn through them for hanging.

More to Do

1. Paint the bag with tempera or craft paint.

2. Fold the center sides in half and cut symmetrical shapes along the fold.

3. Use stickers, sequins, glitter pens, or fabric trim to decorate the mobile.

4. Place an uncut bag of a different color inside the bag with the cutout shapes.

5. Make a lantern or luminaria: Turn the bag over; cut lines or shapes around the opening of the bag; put about 1/2" of sand in the bag; add a tea light.

6. Make mobiles to decorate your classroom for different festivals of the church year or for the students to take home.

Necklace

What You Need

Lunch bag
Scissors
White glue
Water
Brush
Markers
Yarn
Hole punch

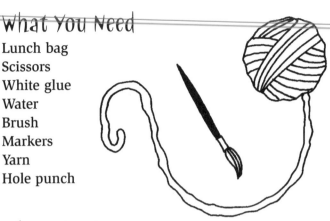

What You Do

1. Cut three or more paper rectangles. Brush a mixture of equal parts glue and water over each of the rectangles then glue them together. Brush the glue mixture over the top rectangle and let it dry.

2. Draw a cross shape on the glued rectangles and cut it out. Punch a hole at the top.

3. Cut a piece of yarn for a necklace and thread it through the hole for a hanger.

4. Cut paper strips about 1/4" to 1/2" wide and 3 or 4 inches long. Make beads by rolling strips around a pencil and gluing the end in place. Decorate with markers. Thread beads onto yarn on each side of the cross.

5. When the desired number of beads has been added, tie the ends of the yarn and wear the necklace.

More to Do

1. Make beads from different colored paper bags.

2. Add wooden beads or dry cereal to the necklace.

3. Instead of yarn, thread beads on plastic or leather lacing.

4. Brush beads with the glue and water mixture. When dry, decorate with permanent markers.

5. Instead of a cross, use one of the optional patterns on pages 56 and 58.

6. Have children make take-home necklaces illustrating a lesson theme or application.

The Lesson Connection

Peter's Confession of Christ: Luke 9:18–27

"Who do you say I am?" Jesus asked His disciples. "You are the Christ," Peter answered. This was no simple statement. Peter publicly confessed his belief that Jesus was no mere teacher but that He was the fulfillment of the Old Testament prophecies of the Messiah. Make a cross necklace to wear to show that you believe that Jesus is the Christ, your Savior from sin.

Other Lesson Connections

Love one another (heart)
Baptism (dove or shell)
Fishers of men (fish)

Palestinian House

What You Need

Brown paper bag
Scissors
Markers or crayons

What You Do

1. Place the flat paper bag in front of you with the fold on top.
2. Using the fold line as a guide, cut the top off of the bag.
3. Open the bottom of the bag and turn it upside down.
4. Cut a door in one side of the house.
5. Decorate with windows, bushes, etc.

More to Do

1. Draw Bible figures on the remaining paper and cut them out. For each figure, cut a strip of paper, glue the ends so it forms a circle, and glue the circle at the base of the back of the figure so it will stand. Use the figures and house to act out Bible stories.
2. Glue the house inside a box to make a diorama. Or use it as a prop in a tabletop puppet play.
3. Make a house from a large grocery bag.
4. Make houses for a classroom Palestinian village or as part of a diorama to take home.

The Lesson Connection

House Built upon a Rock: Matthew 7:24–27

Jesus told a story about two houses, one built on a rock and one built on sand. Make two houses to use as props. Place the houses on a table and tell how one house stood firm when the rains came down but the other house did not. Smash one of the houses with your hand. Explain that putting one's trust in Jesus' words is like building a house upon a rock. Have the children make their own bag house to take home and write on it some of Jesus' words that can help them in times of trouble. Sing "The Wise Man Built His House upon the Rock" or "My Faith Is Built on Nothing Less."

Other Lesson Connections

Elijah and the widow
Wise Men
Jesus heals a paralyzed man

Palm Leaf

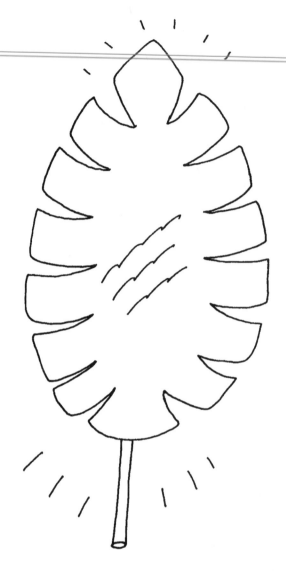

What You Need

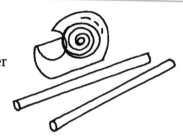

Lunch bag
Scissors
Green crayon or marker
Drinking straws (2)
Tape
Glue

What You Do

1. Flatten the bag in front of you. Cut the two ends of the bag to look like the curved ends of a leaf.

2. Color both sides of the bag green.

3. Tape two straws together to make a long stem. Then glue the stem along the middle of the leaf.

4. Make parallel cuts along each side of the leaf, leaving ¹/₂″ on each side of the center stem.

More to Do

1. Make the palm leaf from a green paper bag, glue green tissue paper over a white bag, or use crayons or tempera to color the bag green.

2. Use a dowel stick instead of drinking straws.

3. Add the palm leaves to a bulletin board or paper banner.

4. Cut palm leaves from large grocery bags. Make a palm tree by sticking the leaves in the top of a cardboard tube wrapped with masking tape.

5. Use palm leaves for a room decoration, visual aid, or as a craft project for children to wave during your worship time.

The Lesson Connection

Palm Sunday: Matthew 21:1–11

"Hosanna" is taken from a Greek word meaning "save now." The people waved palms and cried "Hosanna to the Son of David." Jesus entered Jerusalem as a hero; He left as a criminal, the willing sacrifice for the world's sins. Make a palm branch to wave as you sing a "Hosanna" song to Jesus in your classroom worship.

Other Lesson Connections

Use palm leaves as a background when staging classroom plays based on Bible stories.

Piñata

What You Need

Large paper bag
Hole punch
Scissors
Construction paper
Glue
Yarn
Candy

More to Do

1. Cut figures and shapes to glue around the bag.

2. Cut fringes from tissue or crepe paper.

3. Use patterns found elsewhere in this book for shapes to glue to the piñata. (See patterns on pages 56 and 58.)

4. Make piñatas to use in classroom celebrations of major church festivals.

The Lesson Connection

The Wise Men: Matthew 2:1–12

On Epiphany we remember how Wise Men came from a distant land to bring gifts to the baby King and to worship Him. Cut and glue stars onto your piñata and celebrate Epiphany with a game that reminds you of how Jesus came for the children of Mexico, as well as for children all around the world.

What You Do

1. Fold in the top of the bag about 2″. Punch four holes, two on each side, in the top of the bag.

2. Cut strips of construction paper and fringe them.

3. Glue the fringes around the piñata, beginning at the bottom of the bag and overlapping slightly as you work toward the top.

4. Thread and tie yarn through holes at the top of the bag for hanging.

5. Fill the bag with candy and hang it. Following the Mexican custom, have the children take turns trying to tip the piñata with a broomstick to dump out the candy. Children may wear a loose-fitting blindfold.

Other Lesson Connections

Christmas (angel)
Easter (butterfly)

Robe

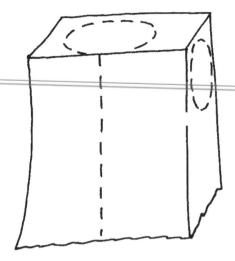

What You Need

Large paper bag
Scissors
Markers or crayons

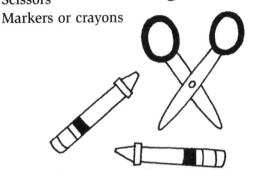

What You Do

1. Cut a slit along the center of the bag. Cut holes for the head and arms.
2. Decorate the robe with brown markers or crayons to simulate animal fur.

More to Do

1. Cut the robe to adapt it to costumes for different characters.
2. Use construction paper, tissue paper, fabric, feathers, cotton balls, or fabric trim to decorate the robe.
3. For a suede effect, crumple the robe and have an adult iron it.
4. Use a large gift bag or a shopping bag for the robe.

The Lesson Connection

John the Baptizer: Luke 3:1–20

Dressed in camel skins, John told the people that the Old Testament prophecies had been fulfilled because the promised Messiah had come. John identified Jesus as the Lamb of God, the one who would be sacrificed for the sins of the world. And John baptized Jesus, marking the beginning of His earthly ministry. Make a paper bag robe, then crumple and iron it. Have a child wear it and pretend to be John, telling the story of his life. Sing "On Jordan's Bank the Baptist's Cry."

Other Lesson Connections

Joseph (Make a coat of many colors.)
Samuel (Make a robe to represent the robe Samuel's mother brought to him each year.)
Christmas (Make shepherds' robes.)
Dorcas (Make purple robes.)
Armor (Make silver or bronze breastplates as the armor of God.)

Rooster

What You Need

Lunch bags (2)
Scissors
Markers or crayons
Construction paper (optional)
Newspaper
Glue
Red tissue paper

What You Do

1. Fold the bag flat in front of you and place your hand on the bag so your fingers are at the top. Draw tail feathers by tracing the tips of your fingers. Cut along the outline, being careful to cut through only one side of the bag.

2. Cut down the four corners of the bag about half way down the bag.

3. Fold down the sides and back of the bag, then trim the sides to form the rooster's wings and tail.

4. On the front of the bag, draw the outline of a rooster head and cut it out. (Optional: Use the pattern on page 64.)

5. Color two eyes and a beak. (Optional: Cut a construction paper beak. Fold the beak in half and glue the bottom half to the head.) Color the rest of the rooster as desired.

6. Crush newspaper and fill the second bag about half way. Fold over the top of the bag and glue it down. Place the bag upside down inside the body of the rooster.

7. Leave the head standing up and fold back the rest of the front to form the top of the rooster. If needed, cut a strip of paper to roll up and glue behind the head as a brace.

8. Cut two strips of red tissue paper. Gather one piece and glue it to the top of the rooster's head for a comb. Gather and glue the other strip below the rooster's beak for a wattle.

More to Do

1. Cut wing, tail, and head sections from construction paper using the patterns on page 64.

2. Glue on movable craft eyes, real feathers, or other craft materials.

3. Adapt the rooster to make a teaching aid for one of several Bible passages mentioning birds or chickens. Let the students make one to take home.

The Lesson Connection

Peter Denies Jesus: Matthew 26:31–35; 69–75

"Before the rooster crows twice," Jesus told Peter, "you will deny Me three times." Even faithful Peter disowned Jesus, leaving Him alone to face His trials and crucifixion. Make a rooster and write "Be Faithful" on it as a reminder to try to stay faithful to Jesus, your Savior. Explain to children that Jesus died for Peter's sins and forgave him. He died for their sins and forgives them too.

Other Lesson Connections

As a hen gathers her chicks around her, so Jesus said, He wants to gather the children of Jerusalem to His side. (Make a hen.)

The ten lepers (Make a Thanksgiving turkey.)

God cares for the birds and He cares for us. (Create a favorite kind of bird.)

Sandal

What You Need

Large brown bag
Scissors
Pencil
Glue

What You Do

1. Cut along the seam of the paper bag, then cut off the bottom of the bag to make a long rectangle.
2. Trace your foot and cut it out to make the sole for a sandal.
3. Cut a strip of paper and glue it to the sole as a strap for the sandal.

More to Do

1. Omit the strap and use markers or crayons to draw a picture of the top of your shoe on the foot shape. Optional: Punch holes and add a shoestring.
2. Make a bulletin board or classroom banner by gluing one or more footprints to a large sheet of paper. Write an appropriate Bible verse or phrase onto the paper.
3. Glue footprints to cardboard and wear the sandals as part of a biblical costume.

The Lesson Connection

Jesus Calls His Disciples: Mark 4:18–22

"Follow Me," said Jesus to Peter and the other disciples; and they did. They left their jobs, families, and homes to follow Jesus' footsteps and spread the Gospel message of salvation through faith in Christ. Make a sandal to remind you that Jesus also calls us to follow Him. Write the words "(Your Name) Follows Jesus" on the sandal. Lead the children in a song or hymn, such as "Let Us Ever Walk with Jesus," "Hark, the Voice of Jesus Calling," or "This Little Gospel Light of Mine."

Other Lesson Connections

Moses and the burning bush
(Use this for a costume.)
Jesus forgives Peter

Scroll

What You Need

Paper bag
Scissors
Markers or crayons
Dowel or craft sticks (2)

The Lesson Connection

Philip and the Ethiopian: Acts 8:26–40

God worked through Philip to explain the Scriptures to a man from Ethiopia. Make a scroll and write words from Isaiah 53 onto it. Use the scroll to act out the story. Explain to students that Philip is an example to all Christians to share their faith in Jesus as the promised Lamb of God for all people.

Other Lesson Connections

Josiah finds the book of the Law

Luke wrote about Jesus; write your own "scroll" about Jesus.

Write and illustrate favorite Bible passages on a scroll.

Create a time line of Jesus' life on a scroll.

What You Do

1. Cut along the seam of the bag, then cut off the bottom to make a long strip. If desired, shorten the height of the strip.

2. Decorate the strip with pictures or the words of a Bible verse.

3. Glue a dowel or craft stick to each end of the paper. Roll each side of the scroll toward the center.

More to Do

1. For a parchment or leather effect, crumple the paper, then iron it before gluing on the dowel or craft sticks.

2. Glue pictures or lesson leaflet pages to the scroll.

3. Use stickers, fabric trim, or glitter to decorate the scroll.

4. Make a scroll for a visual aid when telling Bible stories or as a student project illustrating a specific Bible verse.

Sheep

What You Need

White lunch bag
Scissors
Pencil
Cardstock or poster board
Glue
Cotton balls

What You Do

1. Cut the bag in half.

2. Use a pencil to draw a leg along each corner. Draw the sheep head on one of the shorter sides of the bag. (See illustration.)

3. Cut around the sheep's legs and head.

4. Cut four strips of cardstock as long as each leg and glue a strip inside the legs to strengthen them.

5. Stand the sheep and glue cotton balls over the body.

More to Do

1. Vary the leg length and head to make other animals.

2. Use movable craft eyes.

3. Roll pieces of newspaper to glue behind the sheep's legs to strengthen them.

4. Use the sheep's head pattern on page 60.

5. Make a sheep to use as a classroom puppet or as a take-home project.

The Lesson Connection

The Lord Is My Shepherd: Psalm 23

"The Lord is my Shepherd," wrote David. Have the children make a sheep to remind them that Jesus, the Good Shepherd, leads them and takes care of them each day.

Other Lesson Connections

Parable of the lost sheep
Song: "I Am Jesus Little Lamb"
Jesus is the Lamb of God.

Shoulder Bag

What You Need
Large paper bag
Pencil or marker
Scissors
Glue

The Lesson Connection

Parable of the Sower: Matthew 13:3–30

Jesus used the story of a man sowing seeds to talk about the ways God's Word is received. Make a bag to use in telling this story. For a lesson application, write different witnessing situations on slips and put them in the bag for children to choose and act out. Let the children make a "Sower Bag" from a small paper bag, then fill it with Bible passages to sow the seed of God's Word with others. Write "Sow the Seed" on the bag.

What You Do

1. Draw a line several inches above the bottom of the bag all the way around. This will form the bag "pocket." If desired, draw a flap on one side of the bag.

2. On the middle of two opposite sides of the bag, draw two parallel lines to form the bag strap.

3. Cut out the shoulder bag and glue the top edges of the straps together.

Other Lesson Connections

David and Goliath (Make a small bag to hold David's stones.)

Parable of the good Samaritan (Make a bag to hold the good Samaritan's money.)

More to Do

1. Write an appropriate Bible passage or phrase onto the bag.

2. Use the bag as a storytelling aid. Or have children make a bag to fill with Bible passages or child evangelism materials to give out in a witness situation.

45

Stick Puppet

What You Need

Lunch bag
Markers or crayons
Newspaper
Dowel
Yarn or string
Construction paper
Scissors
Glue

What You Do

1. Draw a face on one side of the paper bag.
2. Stuff the bag with newspaper.
3. Insert the dowel into the bag and tie it in place.
4. Cut strips of construction paper and glue them to the bag for hair. If desired use the edge of the scissors to "curl" the hair.

More to Do

1. Glue yarn, craft hair, or cotton onto the puppet for hair or a beard.
2. Cut facial features from construction paper or paint them on with tempera.
3. Glue on movable eyes.
4. Make stick puppets to use in telling a variety of Bible stories. Have children make puppets to use in applying the story to their life situations.

The Lesson Connection

Joseph in Egypt: Genesis 41–45

Make a stick puppet with fringed black hair to represent Joseph. Use the puppet to tell how Joseph forgave his brothers, explaining that God had turned the evil they did into good. Discuss with students how we receive forgiveness—through Jesus Christ, who took away all of the world's sin. Because of Jesus' death on the cross and resurrection from the grave, God the Father sees us through His righteousness.

Other Lesson Connections

Use puppets to represent Bible characters.
Use puppets to represent contemporary children for lesson applications.

What You Need

Lunch bag
Markers or crayons
Newspaper
Glue

What You Do

1. Flatten the bag in front of you and draw a Bible character or scene.

2. Stuff the bag with newspaper.

3. Glue the top of the bag together, fold it back, and glue it down.

More to Do

1. Use construction paper, fabric, or fabric trim to add details.

2. Draw scenes from a Bible story on each side of the bag. Turn the bag as you tell the story to show what happens next.

3. Use bags in a variety of sizes and colors.

4. Glue several inches together at the top of the bag. Fold down the top to make a flap that hides part of the picture. Draw or glue figures onto the bag, or glue on pictures from a Sunday school lesson leaflet or coloring book. Lift the flap to conclude the story.

5. Leave the top of the bag open. Place items inside to pull out as you tell the story.

6. Make a bag for teaching the lesson. Then have the children make one like it to use in telling the story to someone else.

The Lesson Connection

Ascension: Acts 1:1–11

When Jesus returned to heaven, He rose up into the sky until a cloud hid Him from view. Make a two-sided teaching aid: Make two copies of the pattern for Jesus (page 59). Place Jesus on the mountain on one side of the bag and in the sky on the other side. Glue cotton balls on the flap to make clouds. Show Jesus on the hill, then turn the bag to show Him ascending. Fold over the flap at the point in the story where a cloud hides Jesus from view. Lift the flap to show Jesus again as you remind students that He will come again one day to take them to live in heaven with Him and the heavenly Father. Explain that Jesus comes to us today through His means of grace: the Word of God, Holy Baptism, and the Lord's Supper.

Other Lesson Connections

The fiery furnace

Jonah

Christmas

The prodigal son

Easter

Stuffed Fish

Lunch bag
Markers or crayons
Newspaper
Rubber band
Scissors
Construction paper
Glue

What You Do

1. Draw a fish on the bag. Add eyes, a mouth, and gills with markers or crayons.

2. Stuff the bag with newspaper. Use the rubber band to tie off a tail about two inches from the end of the bag.

3. Cut one top fin and two bottom fins from construction paper. Glue on the fins.

More to Do

1. Before stuffing the fish, punch holes at the top and tie yarn through for a hanger.

2. Before stuffing, add scales with markers, crayons, or tempera paint.

3. Use a colored bag.

4. Glue on sequins, movable eyes, or other craft decorations.

5. Write an appropriate Bible passage or phrase on the fish.

6. Use as a visual aid or storytelling puppet for a lesson in which fish or fishing play a part. Let children make a fish to take home as a reminder of the day's lesson.

The Lesson Connection

Jonah: Jonah

Jonah spent three days inside a big fish before being sent on his way to tell the wicked people of Nineveh of God's love and promises for them. Make a fish to use in telling this story. Make a small figure to represent Jonah (pattern on page 59). Optional: Cut out two figures and glue them together with a ball of cotton in between. Explain to students that this is not a fictional story. Remind them that God worked through Jonah to tell others of His faithfulness; He works through us too. If children are old enough to understand, draw parallels between Jonah and Jesus.

Other Lesson Connections

Creation
Jesus calls fishermen to be His disciples
The great catch of fish
Feeding the 5,000

Stuffed Heart

What You Need

Large paper bag
Scissors
Markers or crayons
Glue stick
Newspaper
Clothespin

The Lesson Connection

Love One Another: John 13:34

Jesus tells us to love one another as He has loved us. Have the class make a decorative stuffed pillow to put in their rooms as a reminder of this command of Jesus. Sing "They'll Know We Are Christians by Our Love." Explain that we cannot keep this command perfectly—but we can know that Jesus kept it perfectly for us. Lead students in a prayer thanking God for loving us so much that He sent Jesus to take the punishment for our sin and to be our righteousness.

Other Lesson Connections

Noah (Ark)
Good Samaritan (heart)

What You Do

1. Cut along the seam of the bag and cut off the bottom to make a large rectangle.

2. Fold the rectangle in half and draw a heart on it.

3. Cut out the hearts and decorate them with markers or crayons.

4. Glue the edges of the hearts together, leaving several inches open for stuffing.

5. Crumple newspaper and carefully push it through the opening. When finished, glue the hole shut and use the clothespin to clamp it together while drying.

More to Do

1. Paint the shape with tempera paint.

2. Use a tapestry needle and yarn, twine, or raffia to sew the shapes together.

3. Write an appropriate Bible passage or phrase onto the shape.

4. Instead of gluing the sides together, staple them.

5. Use one of the other shapes or symbols in this book. (See patterns on pages 56 and 58.)

6. Have students make stuffed shapes for lesson applications.

49

Stuffed Puppet

What You Need

Paper bag
Markers
Newspaper
Rubber band
Tape
Construction paper
Scissors
Plastic knife
Glue

What You Do

1. Flatten the bag and place it in front of you with the open end pointing toward the top of your work area.

2. Using markers draw a line separating the head and body. Draw and color the puppet's face and clothes.

3. Stuff the body with newspaper and section off with a rubber band. Then stuff the head and tape the top of the bag closed.

4. Cut strips of construction paper to glue on for hair. To add curl, pull the paper strips over the dull edge of a plastic knife.

5. Glue on other details cut from construction paper.

6. Place the figure on a flat surface and move it around as you tell the story.

More to Do

1. Duplicate the patterns on pages 59—63 to color, cut out, and glue onto the heads of teaching puppets.

2. Glue fabric or wallpaper over the body. Add other decorative trim as desired.

3. Roll construction paper tubes and glue them to the sides of the figure to make arms.

4. Glue on yarn for hair or use craft hair.

5. Write an appropriate Bible verse or phrase onto the figure.

6. Use puppets for teaching. Have students make a puppet to help them tell the story to someone else.

The Lesson Connection

Jesus and the Children: Mark 10:13–16

"Let the children come to Me," said Jesus. He brought a young child to His side to show His disciples that all people, even children, are called into God's family through Holy Baptism. Have children make figures representing themselves. Have each child write "Jesus loves (name)" on their figure before taking it home.

Other Lesson Connections

Samuel
David and Goliath
Daniel in the lions' den
Have children make puppets to act out contemporary lesson applications.

Tower or Fortress

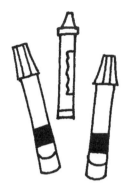

What You Need
Brown paper bags (2)
Scissors
Markers or crayons
Newspaper
Glue

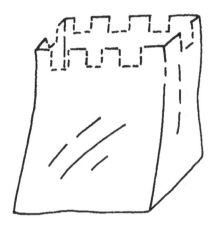

The Lesson Connection

The Lord Is My Fortress: Psalm 18

These words based on Psalm 18:2 remind us that we can look to the Lord God for help in time of trouble. Have the students make a tower and write on it the words of the psalm. As they work, encourage them to tell of times of trouble or danger in their lives when God kept them safe. The psalm is about victory over David's enemies. Ask children to list enemies that may threaten them. Then discuss how Jesus defeated our greatest enemies through His death and resurrection on our behalf.

Other Lesson Connections

Tower of Babel (Attach two bags together to make a taller tower.)
Solomon's temple
Jericho
Buildings in Jerusalem

What You Do

1. Trim the bags to the height desired.

2. Cut out squares from the top of one bag. (See diagram.)

3. Use markers or crayons to draw a door on the fortress and rock shapes around it.

4. Stuff the other bag with crumpled newspaper, fold over the end, and glue it upside down inside the decorated bag.

More to Do

1. Write an appropriate Bible verse or hymn title, such as "A Mighty Fortress Is Our God," on the bag.

2. Cut stone shapes from brown or gray construction paper and glue them onto the bag.

3. Cut around three sides of the door so it opens. Write a verse or hymn title inside the door.

4. Make a large fortress as a classroom visual aid. Then have the children make a small fortress for a lesson application to take home.

Tree or Bush

What You Need

Brown paper bag
Glue
Small paper plate
Green tissue paper

What You Do

1. Cut one or two slits halfway down each side of a paper bag to form tree limbs. As desired, cut additional slits halfway down each branch for shorter branches.

2. Glue the base of the tree to a small paper plate.

3. Leaving the bottom of the bag for the trunk, twist the bag to form the tree limbs and branches.

4. Cut or tear small pieces of green tissue, crumple them, and glue them to the tree for leaves and to the paper plate for grass.

More to Do

1. Stuff the trunk with newspaper to make it wider and sturdier.

2. Glue natural objects such as small stones or dried flowers around the base of the tree.

3. Add figures made from paper or chenille sticks.

4. Use markers or crayons to color the tree or to write an appropriate Bible passage onto its base.

5. Make a large tree and attach it to a bulletin board.

6. Make trees to use with classroom puppet stages.

7. Make trees to add to Bible story dioramas.

The Lesson Connection

Zacchaeus: Luke 19:2–10

"Come down," called Jesus to Zacchaeus, the tax collector. Children are enthralled with this story of the short man who climbed a tree for a better view of Jesus. Use this craft, along with the song, "Zacchaeus," to teach children that Jesus came to forgive and save everyone, even sinful tax collectors. Make pipe cleaner puppets to use in acting out the story, or use the figures provided on page 57.

Other Lesson Connections

The fall of man
Moses and the burning bush
"He is like a tree planted by streams of water." Psalm 1:3
Parable of the mustard seed
Jesus in Gethsemane

Windsock

What You Need

Paper bag
Scissors
Markers
Construction paper
Glue
Hole punch
Yarn

What You Do

1. Cut off the bottom of the paper bag to make a sleeve.

2. Flatten the bag and decorate the sides with markers.

3. Cut construction paper strips and glue them along the bottom of the bag.

4. Use a hole punch to make two holes at the top of the bag. Tie on a length of yarn for a hanger.

5. Hang the windsock.

More to Do

1. Decorate the bag with stickers or designs cut from construction paper.

2. Glue on sequins, glitter, or fabric trim.

3. Glue on strips cut from tissue paper or ribbon.

4. Make windsocks to use as classroom decorations for different seasons and festivals of the church year. (See patterns on pages 56 and 58.)

5. Make windsocks as take-home projects illustrating a Bible story or its application to daily Christian life.

The Lesson Connection

Pentecost: Acts 2

With the sound of rushing wind, flames of fire appeared on the heads of Jesus' disciples. The Holy Spirit had come, just as Jesus had promised! Now the apostles could begin their ministry and spread the Gospel throughout the world. Glue a red paper flame onto each side of a white bag and hang red tissue strips from it. Use metallic or glitter fabric paint to write the words "Come Holy Spirit" on the flame.

Other Lesson Connections

Noah (ark and rainbow)
Good Samaritan (heart)
Baptism (dove)
Trinity (triangle)

Wrapping Paper

What You Need

Large paper bag
Scissors
Markers, crayons, or gel pens
Cookie cutters

What You Do

1. Cut along the seam of the bag. Cut off the bottom of the bag to make a long rectangle.

2. Lay the rectangle in front of you and trace cookie cutter shapes over it.

3. Color in shapes.

4. Use markers or crayons to add additional details.

More to Do

1. Use cookie cutters to stamp tempera paint onto the wrapping paper. Or cut stamp shapes from kitchen sponges, potatoes, or craft foam.

2. Use commercial stamps and a stamp pad for stamping.

3. Write Bible passages and phrases on the paper.

4. Decorate the paper with glitter glue, sewing notions, or other decorative materials.

5. Use shape patterns on pages 56 and 58.

6. Have students make paper to wrap gift items that are part of a class mission project.

The Lesson Connection

Christmas: Luke 2

At Christmas we celebrate God's gift of His Son, our Savior. Giving gifts to others is one way we can respond to God's gift to us—forgiveness and salvation through Jesus Christ, the promised Messiah. Trace or stamp shapes from Christmas cookie cutters to make wrapping paper. Optional: Use ornament patterns found on pages 56 and 58.

Other Lesson Connections

Make wrapping paper for Easter, Baptism, or birthday gifts.

Wreath

The Lesson Connection

**God Cares for the Birds
and Flowers: Luke 12:22–34**

"God, who cares for the birds and flowers, cares for you," Jesus reminded His followers. Have the students in your class make a wreath celebrating God's love and care for them by using a brightly colored bag then adding flower and bird stickers to it. (Optional bird and flower patterns are provided on page 58.) Hang the words "God Cares for (name of child)" in the center of the wreath. Remind students that no matter what happens to us, God has provided for us through Jesus' righteousness.

Other Lesson Connections

Creation (Add animal stickers.)
Lent (Hang a cross in the center of the wreath.)
Easter (Attach butterfly stickers to the wreath.)
Trinity (Add a symbol for each Person of Trinity.)

What You Do

1. Cut along the seam of the paper bag. Cut off the bottom to make a rectangle.
2. Twist the paper rectangle and glue the ends together.
3. Cut construction paper shapes and glue them around the wreath.

More to Do

1. Use tempera paint to paint the wreath green.
2. Wad colored tissue into balls and glue them to the wreath.
3. Wrap the wreath with raffia or ribbon.
4. Glue pictures or stickers to the wreath.
5. Add candle shapes cut from construction paper to make an Advent wreath.
6. Make a storytelling wreath with pictures, stickers, or symbols that tell a Bible story. Or make a wreath that contains a Bible passage or phrase.
7. Use a gift bag or other bags in a variety of colors to make a wreath.

Patterns

Use a photocopier to enlarge or reduce patterns to achieve the desired size.

manger with straw

four-pointed star

crown

angel

cross

ark

rainbow

Patterns

Use a photocopier to enlarge or reduce patterns to achieve the desired size.

Bible characters

Patterns

Use a photocopier to enlarge or reduce patterns to achieve the desired size.

butterfly

heart

cloud

fish

dove

musical note

flame

five-pointed star

flower

Patterns

Use a photocopier to enlarge or reduce patterns to achieve the desired size.

Cut on the dotted line

Cut on the dotted line

Patterns

Use a photocopier to enlarge or reduce patterns to achieve the desired size.

Cut on the dotted line

Cut on the dotted line

Cut on the dotted line

sheep

Patterns

Use a photocopier to enlarge or reduce patterns to achieve the desired size.

Cut on the dotted line

donkey/horse

Cut on the dotted line

camel

Cut on the dotted line

lion

Patterns

Use a photocopier to enlarge or reduce patterns to achieve the desired size.

Patterns

Use a photocopier to enlarge or reduce patterns to achieve the desired size.

Patterns

Use a photocopier to enlarge or reduce patterns to achieve the desired size.

rooster

helmet